COUNTRIES  OF THE WORLD

Ronda Armitage

with photographs by Chris Fairclough

Illustrated by Stefan Chabluk

Wayland

Titles in this series

Australia	India
Canada	New Zealand
The Caribbean	Pakistan
France	The U.S.A.
Great Britain	West Germany

Cover Queenstown, beside beautiful Lake Wakitipu in the South Island, welcomes winter skiers as well as summer tourists.

Opposite In New Zealand, sheep out-number people by about 25 to 1. Motorists often come across sheep being driven along country roads.

First published in 1988 by
Wayland (Publishers) Ltd
61 Western Road, Hove
East Sussex BN3 1JD, England

© Copyright 1988 Wayland (Publishers) Ltd

Editor: Philippa Smith
Series design: Malcolm Smythe
Book design: Force 9

British Library Cataloguing in Publication Data
Armitage, Ronda
    New Zealand. — (Countries of the world).
    1. New Zealand — Juvenile literature
    I. Title II. Series
    993.103'7   DU408

    ISBN 1-85210-053-2

Typeset by Direct Image Photosetting, Burgess Hill,
West Sussex
Printed in Italy by G. Canale and C.S.p.A.
Bound in Belgium by Casterman S.A.

Contents

All words that appear in **bold** in the text are explained in the glossary on page 46.

1 Introducing New Zealand

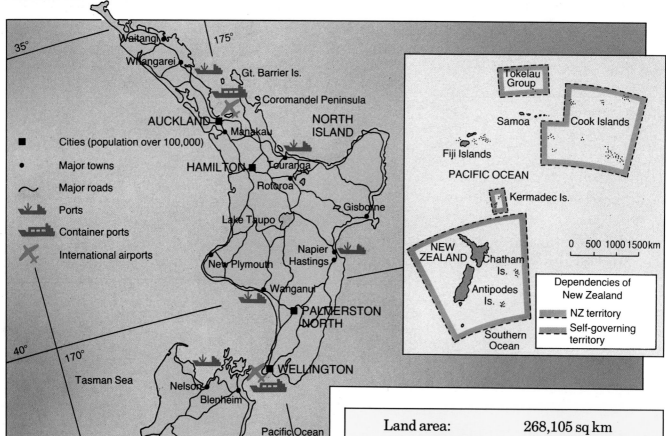

Cities (population over 100,000)

• Major towns

Major roads

Ports

Container ports

International airports

Dependencies of New Zealand
NZ territory
Self-governing territory

Land area:	268,105 sq km
Ross Dependency: (Antarctica)	414,400 sq km
Population:	3,279,500 (1987)
Capital city:	Wellington

NEW ZEALAND'S PLACE IN THE WORLD

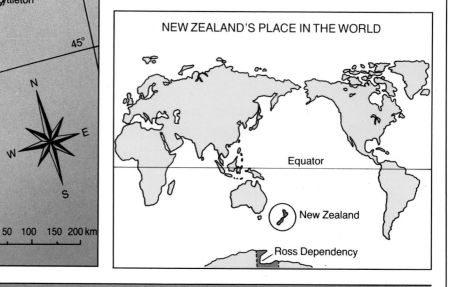

New Zealand is a group of islands in the South Pacific, about midway between the equator and the South Pole. It is made up of the North Island, the South Island and the much smaller Stewart Island. There are many other islands scattered around its coastline. New Zealand also controls Ross Dependency in Antarctica.

New Zealand is about the same size as Great Britain or Italy. In 1987 the population was about 3,300,000, compared with 54 million in Great Britain and 56 million in Italy.

The people who have lived in New Zealand for hundreds of years are called the Maori. They left their homes in **Polynesia** in the Pacific Ocean in the fourteenth century and travelled south to settle in New Zealand. Later, in the nineteenth century, Europeans went to New Zealand to build a new life for themselves. Most were from Great Britain. It took the first British settlers 250 days to reach New Zealand by ship; today, London is only 36 hours away by plane. As New Zealand was so far away from the countries the settlers had left behind, they felt very isolated. It was perhaps because of this that the links with Britain have remained strong for so long.

Since the Second World War (1939-45), New Zealand has developed closer links with other countries in the South Pacific. Several of these islands, such as the Tokelaus, Niue and the Cook Islands, used to be ruled by New Zealand. Today they are independent, but the people are still citizens of New Zealand. Many have left the islands to settle there.

New Zealand has also set up defence and trading links with many Pacific and South-east Asian countries. Once Great Britain bought most of New Zealand's produce; now the USA, Australia and Japan are the country's most important trading partners.

The distances on this signpost at Bluff, at the southern end of the South Island, show New Zealand's isolated position.

2 Land and climate

Farming takes place in the valleys between the mountains of the Southern Alps.

Although there are several lowland areas around the coast, New Zealand is known for its beautiful mountains.

The North Island is made up of low mountain ranges and rolling hills. The centre of this island is an area of volcanic activity. The town of Rotorua, for instance, is famous for its bubbling mud pools, hot springs and **geysers**. Further south are the three highest volcanoes. Two of them, Ruapehu and Ngaurehoe, are still active but the third, Tongariro, is now **dormant**. Earthquakes are common in both islands. The most disastrous of these occurred in Napier in 1931 when 255 people died.

In the South Island, there is a mountain range running down the middle of the island called the Southern Alps. The highest peak is Mount Cook which is 3,764 metres high. The Maori call it *Aorangi*, 'The Cloud Piercer'.

Most parts of New Zealand have plenty of rain, especially the west coast. All regions have long hours of sunshine. The northern part of the North Island is warm enough throughout the year to grow bananas, oranges and lemons, while in the southern part of the South Island frosts and light snow are common in winter. Some mountains in the Southern Alps are always snow-covered.

Much of the original evergreen 'bush', made up of **broadleaf trees**, enormous tree ferns, and clinging vines, was cleared. It is now found mainly on land which is too steep for farming. Some of the trees, like the largest kauri, are thought to be 2,000 years old. The kauri tree grows to 55 metres and used to be very popular for building ships and houses. Now the few kauri that are left are protected.

Native 'bush' on the Coromandel Peninsula.

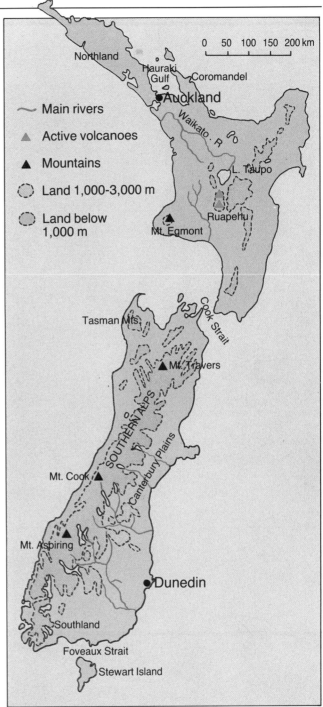

Highest mountain:	Mount Cook	3,764 m
Longest river:	River Waikato	425 km
Largest lake:	Lake Taupo	606 sq km

	Auckland		**Dunedin**	
Average annual rainfall	1268 mm		772 mm	
Average daily temperatures	Max.	Min.	Max.	Min.
January	23°C	16°C	19°C	11°C
July	14°C	8°C	10°C	3°C

3 Wildlife

Above The kiwi is a timid, flightless bird. It is New Zealand's national emblem.

Below The colourful takahe is one of New Zealand's rarest birds.

Many of New Zealand's **native** creatures have strange characteristics. The native frog lays eggs that turn directly into frogs without first becoming tadpoles. The only **reptile**, the tuatara, is a direct descendant of the dinosaur. Many of the birds cannot fly. This is because they had no need to learn to fly to escape their enemies. Until the arrival of humans they had no natural enemies. The largest of these flightless birds was the moa, now **extinct**, which could grow up to 3 metres high. Its kick was powerful enough to kill a man.

When the first settlers reached New Zealand, the only **mammals** they found were two types of bat. As the various peoples visited and settled in New Zealand they took other creatures and plants with them. The Englishman, Captain Cook, took pigs. Some of these pigs escaped into the wild and were never caught. They were known as 'Captain Cookers'. Today, Captain Cookers are hunted both for sport and food. The first European settlers took grasses and trees from Britain, animals such as sheep and cows, and birds such as thrushes and blackbirds.

Some of the animals taken to New Zealand have caused a lot of damage to both the land and the natural wildlife. The government spends thousands of dollars a year controlling deer, rabbit and oppossum. Rats and stoats are particularly harmful to New Zealand's bird life. Today New Zealand takes great

Above The large, lizard-like tuatara may live for 300 years.

Right The pohutukawa tree flowers at Christmas.

care to protect its native species. As well as ten national parks and three maritime parks, many wildlife sanctuaries have been set up on the more isolated islands.

Great efforts are made to keep out dangerous creatures such as snakes and poisonous spiders. A constant watch is kept for destructive diseases such as **foot-and-mouth**. An outbreak of this could be disastrous for New Zealand's farming industry.

4 History

According to a Maori legend, the first voyager to reach New Zealand was a man called Kupe in about AD 950. He named it *Ao-tea-roa*, which means 'land of the long, white cloud'. Following his discovery, wave upon wave of canoes of Maori settlers then travelled the 3,500 or so kilometres to New Zealand. They took with them dogs, rats and edible plants such as the sweet potato. They settled mainly in the warmer North Island in groups known as *iwi*. Each group lived in a village, or *kainga*, which was often near a fortress, or *pa*. Stories of their ancestors were told aloud and learnt by heart as the Maori had no written language.

The first European to discover New Zealand was the Dutch explorer, Abel Tasman, in 1642. But it was not until Captain James Cook made his first voyage in 1769 and made maps of the islands that Europeans came to know about New Zealand.

By 1840 about 2,000 Europeans had settled in New Zealand. They were attracted by reports of the mild climate, fertile land and friendly people. But as more and more people went to New Zealand, so they wanted more land. They tried to take the land belonging to the Maori. In an attempt to solve the problem, the Maori people were persuaded to agree to New Zealand becoming a **colony**, governed by Britain. The Maori promised to sell their land only to Queen Victoria. In return, Britain promised to protect their land

Signing the Treaty of Waitangi – a painting by Marcus King.

The land wars. This nineteenth-century watercolour shows the British attacking a Maori settlement.

and property. The Maori were to have all the rights and privileges of British subjects. This agreement, the Treaty of Waitangi, was signed in February 1840.

Most of the first organized groups of settlers went to the South Island, some to farm and others to look for gold in Otago and Westland. In the North Island settlement happened more slowly.

Despite the Treaty the Government was on the side of the settlers, and during the 1860s the Maori fought the Europeans — or **pakeha** as they called them. The Maori fought desperately for the land they loved but, one by one, the Maori leaders were defeated.

By the 1870s, both the gold rush and the land wars were over. During the next ten years 100,000 settlers arrived. They built roads and railways, cleared land for farms and built homes and schools.

In 1882 the first refrigerated ship, with its cargo of frozen meat, left Dunedin bound for Britain. It was an important event for New Zealand, for it meant that farming produce such as butter, cheese and meat could be sold abroad. Since then, New Zealand has steadily grown into the great farming nation it is today.

This nineteenth-century engraving shows settlers clearing natural woodland to make way for farmland.

During this century the lifestyle of New Zealanders has changed. People have moved from the South Island to the North Island, and from the country to towns. Agriculture is still an important industry, but since the Second World War New Zealand has become a modern industrialized nation. The country has flourished in spite of setbacks, such as the worldwide Depression in the 1930s, when many thousands of people were out of work.

After the Second World War, New Zealand became completely independent from Britain. New Zealand joined Australia as an **ally** of the USA, which had saved both countries from a Japanese invasion during the war. In 1951 a treaty of friendship was signed between Australia, New Zealand and the USA, known as the **ANZUS Pact**.

Although the ties with Britain are less strong now, New Zealand is still a loyal member of the **Commonwealth**. Today the nation sees itself as a vital member of the Pacific community rather than as a 'lonely outpost of the British Empire'.

Right Queen Elizabeth II, the Head of the British Commonwealth, talking to patients at Christchurch Hospital during the Royal Tour of 1954.

Important dates

1100-1350	Arrival of Maori settlers from islands of Central Pacific. This was known as the 'Great Migration'.
1642	European discovery of New Zealand by Abel Tasman.
1769	James Cook's first visit to New Zealand.
1800	Europeans begin to settle in New Zealand.
1840	Treaty of Waitangi signed.
1860-70	Land wars between the Maori people and European settlers.
1863	First major discovery of gold on the west coast of the South Island.
1865	Seat of government moved from Auckland to Wellington.
1877	Education Act provides for free and compulsory education.
1882	First shipment of frozen New Zealand meat reaches Europe.
1893	New Zealand becomes first nation to allow women to vote.
1898	Old-age pensions introduced.
1907	New Zealand becomes a **Dominion**.
1914-18	First World War. 17,000 New Zealand soldiers killed.
1939-45	Second World War. New Zealand soldiers, including famous Maori Battalion, once again fight as part of allied forces. Over 33,000 casualties.
1947	New Zealand becomes fully independent.
1951	Signing of ANZUS Pact.
1984	New Zealand declares itself a **nuclear free zone**.

5 The people today

Although most New Zealanders came from northern Europe, there are now people from all over the world, including Chinese, Asians and Vietnamese. Just under a tenth of the population are Maori. During the nineteenth century, the Maori way of life changed rapidly. European diseases and weapons killed many Maori people and the European lifestyle made it very difficult for them to carry on their traditional way of life. Today, the Maori population is growing once more. Since the Second World War most of the Maori people have settled in the cities. They have had to adapt to European culture and laws. But they try to retain some of their Maori values.

New Zealand is also home to about 90,000 Pacific Islanders, who, like the Maori, have settled mostly in Auckland. Like other settlers before them they hope for a better way of life.

Both the Maori and Pacific Islanders are encouraged to use their own languages as well as English, although English is the official language. New Zealand place names reflect a nation made up of two peoples. Maori place names have a meaning. Probably the longest name in the world is a Maori word, *Taumatawhakatangihanga-koautamateapokaiwhenuakitanatahu*, or 'the hilltop where Tamatea Pokai Whenua played his flute to his loved one.'

Below *Maori women using hot springs to prepare the flax that is used to make traditional Maori skirts.*

Above Pacific Islanders at a Polynesian community market.

Right New Zealanders like to dress casually even for work.

New Zealanders like to think of themselves as direct, out-going, friendly people. The early settlers were determined to create a society in which all people were equal. Today the results of their efforts can still be seen. New Zealand's multi-racial society is probably one of the most successful in the world. It is a society in which there are few poor people or rich people, where everyone has equal rights and opportunities. But it would be untrue to say there is no ill-feeling between the racial groups. Some of the old resentments are still remembered, so **integration** is not always easy.

6 Cities

Freemans Bay in Auckland is a mixture of old and new houses.

Eighty out of every hundred New Zealanders live in cities and towns. Auckland and Wellington, the North Island's largest cities, are both situated beside beautiful, deep-water harbours. They were early settlements which grew up before roads had been built inland, and are still the two largest ports in New Zealand.

Auckland is a colourful city with its mixture of Pacific Island, Maori and European peoples. A quarter of the population of New Zealand live there. It is a pleasant city of wide, tree-lined streets, parks and open spaces. In summer the waters of the Waitemata Harbour are dotted with hundreds of brightly-coloured dinghies, yachts and motor boats.

Wellington is the second largest city. As it is also the nation's capital, Parliament, government buildings and foreign embassies are found there. It is set on steep hills overlooking the harbour entrance, with Cook Strait beyond. The city is nicknamed Windy Wellington, because there are very few days that are wind free. Like San Francisco in the USA, the city is built on an earthquake **fault**. New high buildings are built in a special way to protect them in case of a major earthquake.

About one-third of the South Island's population live in Christchurch, on the edge of the fertile Canterbury Plains. The cathedral in the town square, the River Avon and the parks filled with

Left Lyttleton is the port for Christchurch. Ships bound for Antarctica also sail from here.

Population figures (1987)	
Auckland:	829,000
Wellington:	324,400
Christchurch:	299,400
Dunedin:	106,600

daffodils in springtime are all reminders that this city was designed in England. Unfortunately many buildings face south because the planners forgot that buildings in the southern hemisphere need to face north to get the sun!

Below New high-rise office blocks in Wellington.

Above Otago University in Dunedin.

Dunedin was originally a Scottish settlement. Many of the streets have Scottish names and one of the main landmarks is a statue of Robert Burns, the Scottish poet. During the gold rush days of the 1800s Dunedin grew to be a wealthy merchant and banking town. Gradually the people have moved to the north, and Dunedin is best known now for its university and medical school.

7 Family life

Most *pakeha* families have a mother, father and two or three children and live in a spacious three- or four-bedroomed house in the **suburbs**. Over two-thirds of New Zealanders own their houses. These are generally single-storied and surrounded by a well-planted flower and vegetable garden. Older style houses or villas are built of wood with a verandah at the front and sides. New houses, often built of brick or breeze blocks, may have an area under the house for the garage and a 'rumpus room', a type of playroom usually for older children. Today, most New Zealanders have a high standard of living.

The family help with household chores.

The family relax in the evening. Television is very popular in New Zealand.

Above *A barbecue in the back garden is fun on summer evenings.*

Right *A mobile library brings books to children in a rural settlement.*

As children take packed lunches to school, dinner at night is the main family meal. Family friends may be invited for dinner too, or for afternoon tea, but they are more likely to drop in for a chat over coffee, tea or a glass of chilled beer. Children who live in remote farming areas may have very few friends of their own age. The sheep stations are often many kilometres apart and far away from the nearest settlement, so a visit to the city is a rare treat.

Above Camping beside one of the many beautiful beaches on the Coromandel Peninsula.

Annual holidays are usually taken during the school summer holidays, from late December to early February. Some families may spend this time at a seaside home called a bach (in the South Island it is called a crib). Other families may go camping in one of New Zealand's many camping grounds. For children in remote areas it may be a time to visit relatives in towns and cities. Nowadays some families may fly to town in their own small planes rather than spend hours travelling in the car.

Maori families are often larger and poorer than *pakeha* families. Uncles, aunts, grandparents and other relations may come to stay with the family for long periods of time. Maori families enjoy sharing what they own and looking after each other.

The communal meeting place for a Maori family is on the *marae*, an area of land with a meeting house. This is where the Maori people feel they can keep their traditions alive. Maori children are taught from a very early age how they should behave in this special place. Today, many *pakeha* families are learning how to behave correctly on the *marae* too. All important events take place here. When someone dies all the relations, adults and children, will come together on the *marae* for the Maori funeral called a *tangi*. According to Maori belief, the spirit stays in the body for three days. During this time someone always stays with the dead person. Many people will sleep and eat on the *marae.* They will feel sad together; perhaps share old stories, but most importantly they will feel what it's like to be a Maori.

Children learning about Maori customs and traditions on the marae.

Below *A traditional Maori welcome at a meeting house.*

8 Education

Children in New Zealand must go to school between the ages of six and fifteen, but most start on their fifth birthday. Nearly half of these children will have been to a kindergarten or a play centre before starting school. There are special pre-school groups for Maori children called *kohanga reo*. Most schools are run by the state, and education is free. Secondary education begins at about the age of thirteen (Form 3). There are also some private schools. These are usually run by religious organizations.

Children who live in remote places, such as lighthouses or high country sheep stations, may not be able to attend ordinary school. These children belong to the Correspondence School which is based in Wellington. In all, there are about 2,000 primary and secondary pupils. The pupils exchange lessons with their teachers by post. They can also listen to and watch the school's daily broadcasts on radio and television. The teachers try to visit pupils and their families at least once or twice a year.

A country primary school. Some country schools may have only one or two classrooms.

Some young people will leave school to look for work as soon as they are fifteen, but most stay on to take the School Certificate exam at the end of Form 5, when they are fifteen or sixteen. Those who want to go on to college or university leave school when they are seventeen or eighteen, after they have taken further exams. There are six universities spread throughout both islands. Two have agricultural colleges attached to them and two have medical schools.

Maori children do not always do as well at school as *pakeha* children, probably because lessons are based on a European lifestyle. However, people are recognizing the need to value and encourage the Maori way of life and the Maori language is now being taught in more and more schools. There is a Maori School Certificate examination, and it is also possible to take a degree in Maori or Maori Studies at five of the universities.

Pacific Islanders also want to make sure that their children understand their own culture. Slowly, changes in the educational system are being made to improve this situation.

Third form college pupils using the class computer.

9 Shopping and food

As New Zealand's towns and cities increase in size, the pattern of where people shop is changing. In the towns, most household shopping is done in supermarkets in suburban shopping centres. The corner 'dairy' is useful for evening and Sunday shopping. It provides a limited range of groceries as well as bread, milk and the daily newspapers.

Above A dairy is the local shop in the city suburbs.

Left The grocer's shop in a small town like Arrowtown carries a wide range of goods.

In the more remote country settlements, a general store sells all kinds of things, from gumboots and garden forks to the delicious ice-cream which both children and adults eat in large quantities.

Shopping hours are also changing. The Monday-to-Friday week, with shops open from 9 am to 5.30 pm for four of the days, and until 9 pm on Friday, is now less usual. Today many shops are open on Saturdays as well. This may be because many women now have jobs outside the home and find shopping during the week too difficult.

Settlers from other countries have introduced their own special foods. **Taro** and **yams** from the Pacific Islands, and pasta and salami from Italy, are no longer regarded as unusual foreign foods.

New Zealand also has its own specialities. There are fat, juicy Bluff oysters from Foveaux Strait, tiny fish called whitebait from Westland rivers, and, for a very special occasion, crayfish (rock lobsters). Mutton birds from Stewart Island and kina (sea eggs) are perhaps still enjoyed more by Maori people than *pakeha*.

Food gathering expeditions can be fun for all the family. Shellfish are dug from the sand at low tide and mussels can be found around the rocks. Fruit picking on one of the many fruit farms is another favourite outing.

Right *New Zealand currency and stamps. One New Zealand dollar is divided into 100 cents.*

Below *Taro and water-melon both need a warm climate in which to grow.*

10 Sport and leisure

Left A trotting meeting. In New Zealand, horse racing attracts large crowds.

Below The New Zealand rugby team, the All Blacks, beating France in the 1987 World Cup Final.

New Zealanders love the outdoors. The country has a good climate, beautiful countryside and plenty of space for a wide range of pastimes. All kinds of sports are popular. Team games like rugby, hockey, netball, soccer and basketball are played in winter. Tennis, cricket, horse-riding, badminton and golf are enjoyed by both men and women.

There is so much opportunity for taking part in all kinds of sports, it is no wonder that New Zealand has produced so many fine sportswomen and men — people such as Susan Devoy, the women's world squash champion, and John Walker, who until recently held the world record for the mile. The women's netball team have also been world champions, but perhaps New Zealand's best-known sportsmen are the All Blacks, the national rugby fifteen.

Yachting and the sea have been the love of other famous New Zealanders. Between 1975 and 1977, Dame Naomi James sailed single-handed around the world. She was the first solo woman to sail round Cape Horn, the southern tip of South America.

Sport is encouraged from an early age. Most schools have swimming pools and large playing fields. Boys as young as seven years old take part in competition rugby and soccer. In New Zealand people prefer to play sport rather than watch, although national rugby matches and horse racing attract large crowds.

Right In 1987, Chris Dixon and the yacht KZ-7 were cheered by thousands in the America's Cup race.

In summer many New Zealanders head for the sea, lakes or rivers to take part in watersports. People swim, surf, water ski, mess about in boats or just laze in the sun. Some areas which are particularly beautiful have been turned into national parks, such as the Hauraki Gulf Maritime Park, where people are able to go walking, tramping or climbing. Those who want a little more excitement can go mountaineering and skiing in areas such as the Mount Cook National Park. The mountains of the Southern Alps have been the training ground for many well-known mountaineers, including Sir Edmund Hillary. He became famous when, as members of Sir John Hunt's expedition, he and Sherpa Tensing were the first men to reach the top of Mount Everest in the Himalayas.

Below Sailing dinghies and swimmers on the sandy beach at Takapuna, Auckland.

As in many other western countries, health and fitness is now of great concern and jogging seems to have become the national pastime.

Not all leisure time is spent outdoors. New Zealanders also love to watch television and read books. There are many libraries and even small towns have a well-stocked bookshop. Cities are now big enough to offer a wide range of entertainment for young and old alike. Nightclubs, pubs, theatres and restaurants are all very popular.

Above Joggers and serious athletes join in Auckland's annual 'round the bays' run.

White-water rafting on the River Tasman in the Mount Cook National Park.

11 Religion, festivals, holidays

Until the arrival of the Europeans the Maori worshipped many gods. The first missionaries settled in the Bay of Islands in 1814 and tried to convert the Maori to Christianity. They met with little success until the Bible and hymn book were translated into the Maori language.

Religious beliefs	Followers
Anglican (Church of England)	784,000
Presbyterian	586,500
Roman Catholic	495,300
Methodist	153,000
Baptist	67,700
Other religions	339,300

A Maori church at Rotorua on the North Island.

Today many Maori still belong to the traditional Christian churches but the Ratana religion, which is based on the Bible, is popular as well, especially with younger people. Many Pacific Islanders also have a strong Christian faith. Their church services are usually held in their own languages.

The most important New Zealand festivals are traditionally the same as in Britain. Children eat Easter eggs and hot cross buns at Easter, and wait eagerly for presents from Father Christmas on Christmas Day.

They also celebrate the Queen's official birthday in June, but other public holidays are peculiar to New Zealand, such as **ANZAC** Day in April. On ANZAC Day the people who died in the two world wars are remembered at services which are held at dawn all over the country. The signing of the Treaty of Waitangi is commemorated by Waitangi Day on 6 February.

The Agricultural and Pastoral shows, or the A and P shows as they are called, are very popular in New Zealand. They take place all over the country in summer and early autumn. There is a colourful combination of agricultural and fairground entertainments to attract 'townie' and farmer alike. Displays of the latest agricultural inventions and rosette-clad bulls, cows and sheep mix with merry-go-rounds and candy floss. Axemen chop logs in record time and children and adults show off their horseback skills in the show-jumping ring.

Special days for the Maori people are *huis.* A *hui* may be a wedding, funeral or conference held on the *marae*. Some *huis* are serious; others are more cheerful, with speeches, singing and dancing. Food cooked in a the traditional Maori way, in a **hangi**, provides a welcome feast.

Waiting for a show-jumping event at an 'A and P' show.

12 Culture and the arts

For a long time during the nineteenth century there was little interest in the arts. The settlers were too busy clearing the land and building towns. The few painters and musicians there were felt isolated from those working in Europe. Many left New Zealand to join them.

Today some artists still leave. Singers such as Dame Kiri Te Kanawa need to travel abroad to sing with the world's most famous opera companies. But now, more and more artists and writers are staying in New Zealand. The influence of their country shows in their work. Paintings by artists such as Colin McCahon and Sir Toss Woollaston have been inspired by the beautiful countryside. Writers such as Witi Ihimaera and Sylvia Ashton-Warner write about the pleasures and difficulties of living in New Zealand's multi-cultural society. Margaret Mahy is recognized as one of the best writers for children in the world.

Dame Kiri Te Kanawa, the famous opera singer.

When completed, the Aotea Centre in Auckland will have a wide range of cultural activities for all races.

Left *It is important that traditional Maori skills, such as wood carving, should be passed on to young Maori.*

Below *A traditional Maori carving.*

The Queen Elizabeth II Arts Council was set up in the early 1960s to encourage the arts. It gives financial help to professional theatre and dance companies and provides scholarships for talented young artists and musicians. Some of the funds come from **lotteries** such as the weekly Golden Kiwi.

The New Zealand Film Commission, set up in 1978, assists and promotes film making. Films like *Smash Palace* and *Came a Hot Friday* have been shown around the world.

The Broadcasting Corporation is owned by the state and has sixty-three radio stations and two television channels, TV1 and TV2. Almost every household has a television set; watching television is favourite pastime. Each day there is a mixture of locally produced programmes, the news, sports events, chat shows and plays — as well as programmes from abroad such as *EastEnders* and *Dynasty*.

The traditional Maori crafts of weaving and carving are popular. At the Maori Arts and Crafts Centre, near Rotorua, visitors can watch artists and their apprentices and buy their work.

13 NEW ZEALAND
Farming and fishing

The modern way of rounding up cows.

New Zealand's generally mild climate with good rainfall is ideally suited to farming. The grass grows all the year round and animals do not need to be kept inside in the winter. This means that the costs of running a farm are lower than in many European countries. In New Zealand crops are grown, but not on a large scale, and of these, two-thirds are used as fodder for livestock.

Most of the dairy farms are in the North Island. The average farm is about 50 hectares and has about 120 cows. There might also be a few pigs, some sheep, hens and ducks, and the very important farm dog. The farm owner does most of the work himself but may have someone to help with the milking.

Sheep farms are found on the more rugged hill country and high country in both the North and South Islands. There are 73 million sheep; about twenty-five sheep for every New Zealander! Many of the sheep have been specially bred to suit New Zealand's hill country.

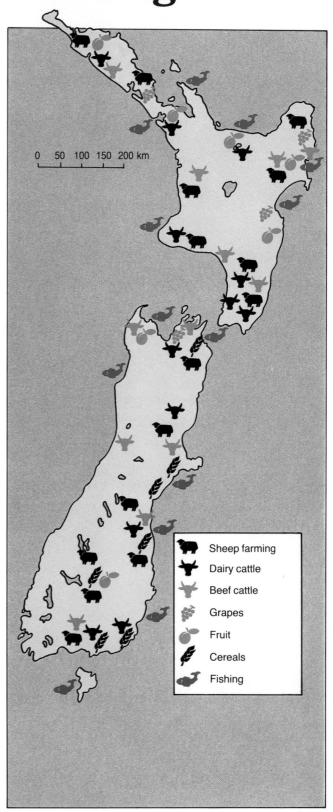

0   50   100 150 200 km

Sheep farming
Dairy cattle
Beef cattle
Grapes
Fruit
Cereals
Fishing

The largest sheep farms, or sheep stations as they are called, are found mainly round the slopes of the Southern Alps in the South Island. These stations are sometimes owned by one family, but more often by large companies. Many stations are so huge that it may take three or four days to round up the sheep and bring them all together in one place. This is called the muster and happens once a year.

Farmers often keep sheep and beef cattle together on the hill country farms. Most of the beef is sold to the USA.

When Britain became part of the **European Economic Community (EEC)** in 1973, the amount of dairy products and meat bought from New Zealand was greatly reduced. New Zealand has had to find other countries to **export** goods to, such as Australia, the USA, Japan and other Asian countries.

Auctioneers at a sheep sale in the North Island. Sheep are raised for their meat and wool.

As well as selling the traditional dairy and meat products abroad, New Zealand has also been successful in selling more unusual products. Avocado pears and kiwi fruit are two examples. These can be grown outside and so growing costs are kept low. Even the cost of sending them by air does not make these fruits too expensive once they reach their European and American markets.

Grapes are also grown and New Zealand wine is now winning international wine medals.

There are 3,000 deer farms in New Zealand. The meat (venison) is sold mostly to the USA. Goat farming has also started recently. The goats are kept for meat and milk. Their luxurious mohair wool is shorn and then sold to the fashion industry.

Above The numbers of deer being farmed are increasing each year.

Below Kiwi fruit must be picked with care. Only the best fruit is exported.

Fishing is also important for New Zealand, although it was not until after 1978 that fish began to be sold abroad in large quantities. In that year New Zealand declared a 320-kilometre Exclusive Economic Zone around the coastline. The number of boats allowed to fish are carefully controlled. A government department also checks that the waters are not being overfished. The Government has encouraged the fishing industry by providing money to buy larger and better-equipped vessels. The larger boats, often jointly owned by local fishermen and foreign companies, may spend many days at sea. Most fish are now caught by **trawlers** in the deeper waters around the coast.

Above A squid boat in Timaru Harbour. Much of this fish goes to Japan and Taiwan.

Right A Maori supervisor in a mussel processing factory.

14 Industry

New Zealand has very few mineral resources; iron and steel are produced from iron ore sands on the North Island's west coast and small quantities of coal are still being mined. Most of the coal is used in homes but a little is sold to Japan and Korea. Recently there has been renewed interest in gold mining.

Large quantities of natural gas have been discovered at Kapuni and offshore Taranaki (the Maui field). This has meant that a whole new range of industries has been developed. For instance, liquid petroleum gas is often used as a cheap alternative to petrol in specially converted motor vehicles. The cost of buying fuel from abroad is very expensive and it is hoped that soon only half the transport fuel needed will come from overseas.

New Zealand is fortunate to have long, fast-flowing rivers suitable for damming. This provides cheap electricity in the form of **hydro-electric** power (HEP). Also, hot steam from the ground at Wairekei provides geothermal power. There is plenty of electricity to supply both homes and industry.

At a smelter at Bluff, bauxite ore imported from Australia is refined into aluminium.

Above Pinus radiata *trees grow very quickly in New Zealand. Here, the trees are thinned to avoid overcrowding.*

Manufacturing and industry are being encouraged so that New Zealand does not have to **import** so many goods. Most household items such as fridges, washing machines and television sets are made in New Zealand. The engineering industries provide much of the machinery needed for agriculture and horticulture. However, New Zealand has no motor industry. Nine-tenths of the cars, mostly from Japan, are brought into New Zealand as parts and assembled in the country.

Much of the land on the North Island's volcanic plateau was thought to be unsuitable for farming. However, exotic forests, mostly *pinus radiata* trees, were planted there in the 1930s and the 1960s. These trees are sent to mills to be made into sawn timber and pulp for the paper industry. To meet the needs of this very important industry, towns such as Kawerau and Tokoroa have been built and a deep water port has been developed at Tauranga.

New Zealand's beautiful scenery attracts visitors from all over the world, especially from Australia, the USA, Japan, Britain and the Pacific Islands. Tourism is becoming another very important industry.

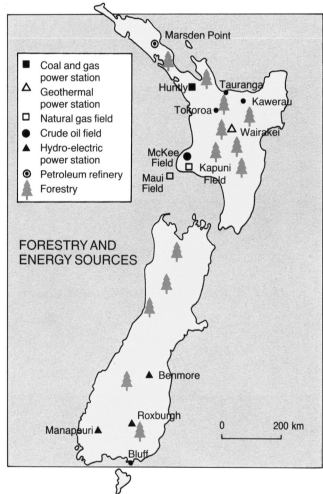

FORESTRY AND ENERGY SOURCES

Main exports:	Meat products, dairy products, wool, forest products, fruit and vegetables
Main imports:	Motor cars, crude oil, iron and steel, refined motor spirits

15 Transport

Above *There are two motorways in New Zealand. This one crosses Auckland, the other goes to Wellington.*

Below *Transporting sheep on a dusty, gravel country road.*

New Zealand is a land of car owners; one car to every two people. New Zealanders can take their driving test at the age of fifteen. The car is the main means of transport for most people, both for work and for pleasure. In spite of the fact that so many people own cars the roads outside the towns are quite empty. The larger cities are beginning to have the same traffic problems as more highly populated countries; long queues during the rush hour, congested city centres and limited space for city parking.

Building the roads and railways in such a mountainous and bush-covered country was a slow and expensive business. Long bridges were needed to cross the many wide rivers, and tunnels were needed when the hills became too steep to climb. Most of the work was done with pick, shovel and wheelbarrow.

The 4,800 kilometres of railway track run mainly from north to south on both islands. The two islands are connected by a roll-on/roll-off ferry service. The use of the railways for both passengers and **freight** has been declining for several years and small railway tracks and stations are being closed.

Air travel is important both for linking remote parts of the country and for maintaining links with the rest of the world. Air New Zealand, the state-owned airline, flies daily to the larger towns and cities and several times a week to London, Europe and the USA. Goods, such as mail, fruit and flowers, which

Above Ski planes transport both people and equipment to snow-covered areas too steep for roads.

require a quick service, are also being carried by plane.

Once, enormous passenger ships called regularly at Wellington and Auckland. Now these ports are used mainly for the important **container ships** that carry New Zealand produce all over the world. In the early days of settlement coastal shipping was the main form of transport around New Zealand. Today, it carries less freight each year.

Right A container ship in Wellington Harbour.

16 Government

New Zealand is an independent member of the British Commonwealth. The Queen's interests in the country are represented by the Governor-General, who is always a New Zealander.

The New Zealand Parliament is unusual as it has only one house, the House of Representatives. There are ninety-five seats in the House. These are occupied by Members of Parliament who each represent one area of New Zealand. Four of the seats are for Maori MPs. This means the Maori people can vote for someone who has their particular interests at heart.

Below The structure of the New Zealand Government.

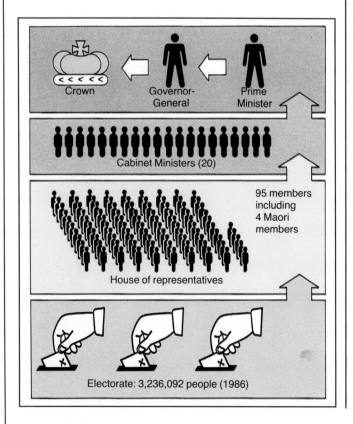

Crown — Governor-General — Prime Minister

Cabinet Ministers (20)

95 members including 4 Maori members

House of representatives

Electorate: 3,236,092 people (1986)

Above The Parliament buildings in Wellington are known as the 'Beehive'.

New Zealand is a parliamentary democracy. This means its citizens can vote freely for one of several political parties. The two main political parties are National and Labour. In 1979 several well-known Maori people formed a new party called *Mana Motuhake*. About one-sixth of the Maori population voted for the party at its first election. Elections are held every three years. People aged over eighteen years may then choose their MP. New Zealanders feel quite close to their politicians, and even the Prime Minister has his phone number in the telephone directory.

New Zealand, like Sweden and Great Britain, is a welfare state. This means that the state takes care of its citizens when they are old or ill or unemployed. The money for this comes from taxes and, like most people, New Zealanders often complain about their high rate of tax!

Many of the big industries and services such as broadcasting, electricity and telecommunications are owned by the state. The state also provides low cost housing, called state housing, for poorer families.

The legal system is based on a mixture of English and Scottish law. About 4,000 policemen make sure that law and order is kept. They do not carry weapons except in emergencies. A separate traffic police force ensures the road laws are kept and conducts driving tests.

Many Maori communities have Maori wardens who help to promote law and order, particularly among the younger people. Because they understand the customs and traditions of their people, they are treated with respect.

Left A Maori warden greets a friend in the traditional way known as hongi.

Below Policemen patrol a pedestrian shopping precinct in Auckland.

17 Facing the future

Recently New Zealand, like many other countries, has had difficult times. Once the nation was proud that anyone who wanted to work could have a job. Today, unemployment is a problem, particularly among young Maori and Pacific Islanders, and the gap between rich and poor people is widening. Many New Zealanders have left to find work in Australia. Some of them are highly-educated, skilled people needed by their country but they prefer the work opportunities available overseas.

Above *A protest march about job losses at one of New Zealand's large meat-freezing works.*

New Zealanders take care to protect their natural environment. This is one of the ten national parks.

New Zealand has always been thought of as a country where all the different nationalities get along very well together. Not all New Zealanders agree with this. The Maori feel that in the past they have had to give up too much of their way of life in order to fit into *pakeha* society. Now they are more sure of themselves; they are determined to play their part as New Zealanders while still keeping the important parts of their Maori culture and traditions. The *pakeha*, too, see that Maori society may offer some different and useful ways for living in the twenty-first century.

New Zealanders are also aware of the need for conservation, not only of their own country and its unique wildlife, but also of Antarctica. New Zealand was one of twelve countries to sign the Antarctic Treaty in 1957, which aims to keep Antarctica for scientific investigation, to protect wildlife, and to ban nuclear tests.

New Zealand has declared itself a **nuclear free zone**, and in February 1985, the New Zealand government refused to let a warship from the USA enter a New Zealand port because that country would not state whether the vessel carried nuclear warheads. Relations between the two countries have been difficult ever since. But many countries congratulated New Zealand for acting against nuclear arms in this way. It seems that today, New Zealanders are confident enough as a nation to tackle such an important issue in spite of strong opposition from one of the world's great powers.

A Maori mother and her little boy in traditional dress. The Maori people are very proud of their culture.

Glossary

Ally   A country, person or group united with another. In the Second World War (1939-45) the Allies were Britain and the Commonwealth countries, the USA, the Soviet Union, France and Poland. They fought against Nazi Germany, Fascist Italy and Japan.

ANZAC   The letters stand for Australian and New Zealand Army Corps. These soldiers fought in Europe during the First and Second World Wars.

ANZUS Pact   The agreement, signed by Australia, New Zealand and the USA in 1951, stating that if any one of the three countries goes to war, the other two will send troops in support.

Broadleaf trees   Trees that have broad rather than needle-shaped leaves.

Colony   A land occupied and governed by people from another country.

Commonwealth   The association of states that are, or have at some time been, ruled by Britain. All the member states regard the British Queen as the Head of the Commonwealth.

Container ships   Specially-designed ships that carry goods which have first been loaded into huge, oblong containers.

Dominion   A name formerly applied to self-governing divisions of the British Empire.

Dormant   Quiet and inactive; used to describe a volcano which is neither extinct nor erupting.

European Economic Community (EEC)   Also called the Common Market, this Western European economic association is made up of twelve countries (including Britain). There is free trade (without taxes) between the countries. Goods bought from outside the EEC are taxed.

Extinct   No longer existing.

Export   To sell goods to a foreign country.

Fault   A break in the Earth's crust which may move during earthquakes.

Foot-and-mouth   A very infectious disease that affects cattle, pigs, sheep and goats.

Freight   Goods sent by air, sea or land.

Geysers   Natural springs which at times send up jets of hot water and steam.

Hangi   A Maori way of cooking food. It is wrapped in leaves and cooked among heated stones in the ground.

Hydro-electric   Producing electricity from water power.

Import   To buy goods from a foreign country.

Integration   Mixing people from different races, religions or cultures with an existing community.

Lotteries   Competitions in which certain tickets win money or prizes.

Mammal   Any of the animals whose females have milk to feed their young (such as humans, sheep or rabbits).

Native   Used to describe a person, creature or plant which is found in a particular country.

Nuclear free zone   In the New Zealand nuclear free zone nuclear weapons are totally banned. They are not stored or tested in New Zealand, and they are not allowed to come to New Zealand in visiting ships or aircraft.

Pakeha   The Maori name for people of other races.

Polynesia   Islands in the Pacific Ocean which include the Cook Islands, Tonga, Samoa, and many others.

Reptile   A cold-blooded crawling or creeping animal with a scaly skin (such as a snake, crocodile or lizard).

Suburbs   An area of housing situated away from a town or city centre.

Taro   A type of root vegetable.

Trawlers   Fishing boats. The fish are caught in a large net which is pulled through deep water behind the trawler.

Yam   A potato-like vegetable.

Books to read

Hall, Peter with Wright, Vernon *A Shepherd's Year* (David and Charles, 1987)

Higham, Charles *The Maoris* (Cambridge University Press, 1981)

King, Michael *New Zealand in Colour* (Reed Methuen, 1986)

Locke, Elsie *The Kauri and the Willow* (P. D. Hasselberg, Government Printer, Wellington, 1984)

Mahy, Margaret *New Zealand Yesterday and Today* (Franklin Watts, 1975)

Pope, Diana and Jeremy *The Mobil Illustrated Guide to New Zealand* (Reed Methuen, 1982)

Robson, Michael *New Zealand in Pictures* (Sterling, 1979)

Sinclair, K., Stenson, M. and Bassett, J. *The Story of New Zealand* (Reed Methuen, 1983)

Wiremu, Graham *The Maoris of New Zealand* (Wayland, 1984)

These and many other books, including children's fiction, are available from The New Zealand Bookshop in London:

Whitcoulls Ltd
The New Zealand Bookshop
Royal Opera Arcade
Pall Mall
London SW1Y 4UY

Tel: 01-930 4587

Further information, including illustrated booklets, maps, posters, films and up-to-date statistics, can be obtained by writing to:

Information Section
New Zealand High Commission
Haymarket
London SW1Y 4TQ

Tel: 01-930 8422

Picture acknowledgements

All photographs were taken by Chris Fairclough with the exception of the following:
Alexander Turnbull Library, Wellington, New Zealand 10, 11, 12; Bruce Coleman Ltd 8 (bottom/John Fennell), 9 (top/John Markham), 17 (centre/G. G. Hunter); Colorsport 26 (right); COMPIX — Commonwealth Institute 30, 35; High Commissioner for New Zealand 8 (top), 15 (top), 23, 29 (top), 33 (top); Axel Poignant Archive 14, 21 (bottom); Popperfoto 13; Sporting Pictures (UK) Ltd 27; TOPHAM 32 (top); Wayland Picture Library 43 (left); ZEFA 45.

Index